Tao

Te

Ching

JEREMY P. TARCHER/PENGUIN
a member of Penguin Group (USA) Inc.
New York

Tao
Te
Ching

❧

LAO TZU

Translated by
JONATHAN STAR

The New Translation from Tao Te Ching: The Definitive Edition

JEREMY P. TARCHER/PENGUIN
Published by the Penguin Group
Penguin Group (USA) Inc., 375 Hudson Street, New York, New York 10014, USA • Penguin
Group (Canada), 90 Eglinton Avenue East, Suite 700, Toronto, Ontario M4P 2Y3, Canada
(a division of Pearson Canada Inc.) • Penguin Books Ltd, 80 Strand, London
WC2R 0RL, England • Penguin Ireland, 25 St Stephen's Green, Dublin 2, Ireland
(a division of Penguin Books Ltd) • Penguin Group (Australia), 250 Camberwell Road,
Camberwell, Victoria 3124, Australia (a division of Pearson Australia Group Pty Ltd) •
Penguin Books India Pvt Ltd, 11 Community Centre, Panchsheel Park, New Delhi–
110 017, India • Penguin Group (NZ), 67 Apollo Drive, Rosedale, North Shore 0632,
New Zealand (a division of Pearson New Zealand Ltd) • Penguin Books (South Africa) (Pty)
Ltd, 24 Sturdee Avenue, Rosebank, Johannesburg 2196, South Africa

Penguin Books Ltd, Registered Offices: 80 Strand, London WC2R 0RL, England

First Tarcher Cornerstone Edition 2008
Copyright © 2001 by Jonathan Star

These translations originally appeared in *Tao Te Ching: The Definitive Edition*, translated by
Jonathan Star (Tarcher, 2001, 2003).

Most Tarcher/Penguin books are available at special quantity discounts for bulk purchase for
sales promotions, premiums, fund-raising, and educational needs. Special books or book
excerpts also can be created to fit specific needs. For details, write Penguin Group (USA) Inc.
Special Markets, 375 Hudson Street, New York, NY 10014.

Library of Congress Cataloging-in-Publication Data

Laozi.
[Dao de jing. English]
Tao te ching : the new translation from tao te ching ; the definitive edition / Lao Tzu ;
translation by Jonathan Star.
p. cm.
Originally published: Tao te ching : the definitive edition, 2001
ISBN 978-1-58542-618-8
I. Star, Jonathan. II. Title.
BL1900.L26E5   2008   2007044948
299'.51482—dc22

Printed in the United States of America
17 19 20 18 16

BOOK DESIGN BY NICOLE LAROCHE

While the author has made every effort to provide accurate telephone numbers and Internet
addresses at the time of publication, neither the publisher nor the author assumes any
responsibility for errors, or for changes that occur after publication. Further, the publisher does
not have any control over and does not assume any responsibility for author or third-party
websites or their content

To submit translations, to provide feedback on the material contained in this book, or to
contact Jonathan Star, e-mail: unity@ffc.net or unity10@aol.com

To the one
who shares her purity,
reveals her wonder,
and touches the moon in her dreams.

Contents

Tao
Te
Ching

Introduction

Don't let this little book fool you. It is small in size but it's going to have a great impact on your life. It is a short eighty-one verses but it's going to live a long time in your memory. While you'll be able to apply its meaning to your daily life right away, it will probably take you years to embody.

The Tao Te Ching is a book of ancient Chinese wisdom written around 500 B.C., which by custom is attributed to the great sage Lao Tzu. One reason the Tao Te Ching has endured for thousands of years is because on the surface it appears to be a simple, almost conversational book, which immediately befriends you—but which upon continued reading reveals a timeless brilliancy of wise poetic truths. In truth it is a sacred text of depth and genius that has, in my experience, no equal. The Tao Te Ching is a key—a key that will unlock for you a new way of understanding life and a new way of living yours.

This is *the* translation for anyone truly wanting to understand the Tao Te Ching. Up until recently, this Eastern text has been translated into English by scholars since the late 1800s. While they used the English lexicon to accomplish their purpose (which was to make a scholarly translation), and while it left the text correct in a literal sense, it deprived the verses of their sheer beauty and poetic power. Thus many of these early translations come across as a bit dusty, old-fashioned, and irrelevant to our lives.

Don't take my word for it, see for yourself. First the older translation of the first stanza of Verse 5:

Heaven and Earth are not humane,
And regard the people as straw dogs.
The sage is not humane,
And regards all things as straw dogs.
(Translated by Charles Muller, Tōyō Gakuen University)

Now Jonathan Star's translation:

Heaven and Earth have no preference.
A man may choose one over another
But to Heaven and Earth all are the same
The high, the low, the great, the small—
All are given light
All get a place to rest

The first is an accurate translation that might be intellectually correct. Jonathan Star's translation also adheres closely to the original text, but is far more profound because of its ability to be immediately grasped and applied to your life. Scholarly texts feed the mind and that's a good thing; but a text that feeds the mind, body and soul, and, not to mention, one which can help us to transform our lives today, is infinitely more valuable.

While the early translations are still common fare and have value for the scholar, a recent number of modern translations have emerged that appeal to the spiritual seeker. Those translations (or "versions")—by Stephen Mitchell, Ursula Le Guin, and Brian Browne Walker, just to name a few—all offer something of value, and I've admired many of them. However, none of them have done what Jonathan Star has done, which is to marry the scholarly concerns of accuracy with the poetry of someone who has lived the words. He brilliantly balances the two worlds—the academic and the experiential—in a way that I believe no other translator of the Tao Te Ching has done before him. For me, this is simply the best translation available, bar none.

Here's what you can expect. I have been a teacher of the Tao for nearly two decades, and since the day this text was put into my hands I have been teaching from it exclusively. It has brought me and thousands of my students over the years the pure and simple heart of the Tao Te Ching; and as a result it has fed our hunger, quenched our thirst, and ignited our desire to live our everyday lives in new ways—simply, deeply, richly, fully, meaningfully. I believe this translation of the Tao

Te Ching will lead you into a personal, direct, and even mystical experience of the Tao, which will uplift and transform your life in countless ways. Expect it to engage you not only intellectually, but emotionally, mentally, and spiritually. To put it even more plainly: this translation will positively change your life.

Believe me—you can trust the translation you are holding in your hands.

—AUGUST GOLD
Sacred Center New York

Verse 1

A way that can be walked
   is not The Way
A name that can be named
   is not The Name

Tao is both Named and Nameless
As Nameless, it is the origin of all things
As Named, it is the mother of all things

A mind free of thought,
   merged within itself,
   beholds the essence of Tao
A mind filled with thought,
   identified with its own perceptions,
   beholds the mere forms of this world

Tao and this world seem different
   but in truth they are one and the same
The only difference is in what we call them

How deep and mysterious is this unity
    How profound, how great!
It is the truth beyond the truth,
    the hidden within the hidden
It is the path to all wonder,
    the gate to the essence of everything!

Verse 2

Everyone recognizes beauty
    only because of ugliness
Everyone recognizes virtue
    only because of sin

Life and death are born together
Difficult and easy
Long and short
High and low—
    all these exist together
Sound and silence blend as one
Before and after arrive as one

名

The Sage acts without action
    and teaches without talking
All things flourish around him
    and he does not refuse any one of them
He gives but not to receive
He works but not for reward
He completes but not for results
He does nothing for himself in this passing world
    so nothing he does ever passes

Verse 3

Putting a value on status
    will cause people to compete
Hoarding treasure
    will turn them into thieves
Showing off possessions
    will disturb their daily lives

Thus the Sage rules
    by stilling minds and opening hearts
    by filling bellies and strengthening bones
He shows people how to be simple
    and live without desires
To be content
    and not look for other ways
With the people so pure
Who could trick them?
What clever ideas could lead them astray?

When action is pure and selfless
    everything settles into its own perfect place

Verse 4

Tao is empty
    yet it fills every vessel with endless supply
Tao is hidden
    yet it shines in every corner of the universe

With it, the sharp edges become smooth
    the twisted knots loosen
    the sun is softened by a cloud
    the dust settles into place

So deep, so pure, so still
    It has been this way forever
You may ask, "Whose child is it?"—
    but I cannot say
This child was here before the Great Ancestor

Verse 5

Heaven and Earth have no preference

A man may choose one over another
    but to Heaven and Earth all are the same
The high, the low, the great, the small—
    all are given light
    all get a place to rest

The Sage is like Heaven and Earth
To him none are especially dear
    nor is there anyone he disfavors
He gives and gives without condition
    offering his treasure to everyone

徼

The universe is like a bellows
    It stays empty yet is never exhausted
    It gives out yet always brings forth more

Man is not like this
When he blows out air like a bellows
    he becomes exhausted
Man was not made to blow out air
He was made to sit quietly and find the truth within

Verse 6

Endlessly creating
Endlessly pulsating
The Spirit of the Valley never dies
She is called the Hidden Creator

Although She becomes the whole universe
    Her immaculate purity is never lost
Although She assumes countless forms
    Her true identity remains intact
Whatever we see or don't see
Whatever exists or doesn't exist
Is nothing but the creation of this Supreme Power

Tao is limitless, unborn, eternal—
    It can only be reached through the Hidden Creator
She is the very face of the Absolute
The gate to the source of all things eternal

Listen to Her voice
    Hear it echo through creation
Without fail, She reveals her presence
Without fail, She brings us to our own perfection

Verse 7

Heaven is ancient
Earth is long-lasting
Why is this so?—
    Because they have no claims to life
By having no claims to life
    they cannot be claimed by death

The Sage puts his own views behind
    so ends up ahead
He stays a witness to life
    so he endures
What could he grab for
    that he does not already have?
What could he do for himself
    that the universe itself has not already done?

Verse 8

The best way to live
    is to be like water
For water benefits all things
    and goes against none of them
It provides for all people
    and even cleanses those places
    a man is loath to go
In this way it is just like Tao

Live in accordance with the nature of things:
Build your house on solid ground
Keep your mind still
When giving, be kind
When speaking, be truthful
When ruling, be just
When working, be one-pointed
When acting, remember—timing is everything

One who lives in accordance with nature
    does not go against the way of things
He moves in harmony with the present moment
    always knowing the truth of just what to do

Verse 9

Grabbing and stuffing—
   there is no end to it

Sharpen a blade too much
   and its edge will soon be lost
Fill a house with gold and jade
   and no one can protect it
Puff yourself with honor and pride
   and no one can save you from a fall

Complete the task at hand
Be selfless in your actions
   This is the way of Heaven
   This is the way to Heaven

Verse 10

Hold fast to the Power of the One
It will unify the body
    and merge it with the spirit
It will cleanse the vision
    and reveal the world as flawless
It will focus the life-force
    and make one supple as a newborn

As you love the people and rule the state
    can you be free of self-interest?
As the gates of Heaven open and close
    can you remain steadfast as a mother bird
    who sits with her nest?
As your wisdom reaches the four corners of the world
    can you keep the innocence of a beginner?

常

Know this Primal Power
    that guides without forcing
    that serves without seeking
    that brings forth and sustains life
        yet does not own or possess it

One who holds this Power
    brings Tao to this very Earth
He can triumph over a raging fire
    or the freeze of winter weather
Yet when he comes to rule the world
    it's with the gentleness of a feather

Verse 11

Wu is nothingness, emptiness, non-existence

Thirty spokes of a wheel all join at a common hub
    yet only the hole at the center
    allows the wheel to spin
Clay is molded to form a cup
    yet only the space within
    allows the cup to hold water
Walls are joined to make a room
    yet only by cutting out a door and a window
    can one enter the room and live there

Thus, when a thing has existence alone
    it is mere dead-weight
Only when it has *wu*, does it have life

Verse 12

The five colors blind the eye
The five tones deafen the ear
The five flavors dull the palate
Racing, hunting, and galloping about
    only disturb the mind
Wasting energy to obtain rare objects
    only impedes one's growth

So the Sage is led by his inner truth
    and not his outer eye
He holds to what is deep
    and not what lies on the surface

Verse 13

"Be wary of both honor and disgrace"
"Endless affliction is bound to the body"

What does it mean,
    "Be wary of both honor and disgrace"?
Honor is founded on disgrace
    and disgrace is rooted in honor
Both should be avoided
Both bind a man to this world
That's why it says,
    "Be wary of both honor and disgrace"

What does it mean,
    "Endless affliction is bound to the body"?
Man's true self is eternal,
    yet he thinks, "I am this body, I will soon die"
This false sense of self
    is the cause of all his sorrow
When a person does not identify himself with the body
    tell me, what troubles could touch him?

One who sees himself as everything
    is fit to be guardian of the world
One who loves himself as everyone
    is fit to be teacher of the world

Verse 14

Eyes look but cannot see it
Ears listen but cannot hear it
Hands grasp but cannot touch it
Beyond the senses lies the great Unity—
    invisible, inaudible, intangible

What rises up appears bright
What settles down appears dark
Yet there is neither darkness nor light
    just an unbroken dance of shadows
From nothingness to fullness
    and back again to nothingness
This formless form
This imageless image
    cannot be grasped by mind or might
Try to face it
    In what place will you stand?
Try to follow it
    To what place will you go?

Know That which is beyond all beginnings
    and you will know everything here and now
Know everything in this moment
    and you will know the Eternal Tao

Verse 15

The masters of this ancient path
  are mysterious and profound
Their inner state baffles all inquiry
Their depths go beyond all knowing
Thus, despite every effort,
  we can only tell of their outer signs—
Deliberate, as if treading over the stones of a winter brook
Watchful, as if meeting danger on all sides
Reverent, as if receiving an honored guest
Selfless, like a melting block of ice
Pure, like an uncarved block of wood
Accepting, like an open valley

調

Through the course of Nature
  muddy water becomes clear
Through the unfolding of life
  man reaches perfection
Through sustained activity
  that supreme rest is naturally found

Those who have Tao want nothing else
Though seemingly empty
     they are ever full
Though seemingly old
     they are beyond the reach of birth and death

Verse 16

Become totally empty
Quiet the restlessness of the mind
Only then will you witness everything
    unfolding from emptiness
See all things flourish and dance
    in endless variation
And once again merge back into perfect emptiness—
    Their true repose
    Their true nature
Emerging, flourishing, dissolving back again
    This is the eternal process of return

To know this process brings enlightenment
To miss this process brings disaster

Be still
Stillness reveals the secrets of eternity
Eternity embraces the all-possible
The all-possible leads to a vision of oneness
A vision of oneness brings about universal love
Universal love supports the great truth of Nature
The great truth of Nature is Tao

Whoever knows this truth lives forever
The body may perish, deeds may be forgotten
But he who has Tao has all eternity

Verse 17

To know Tao alone,
  without trace of your own existence,
  is the highest
Next comes loving and praising it
Then fearing it
Then despising it

萬

If one doesn't trust himself
  how can he trust anyone else?

物

The great ruler speaks little
  and his words are priceless
He works without self-interest
  and leaves no trace
When all is finished, the people say,
  "It happened by itself"

Verse 18

When the greatness of Tao is present
   action arises from one's own heart
When the greatness of Tao is absent
   action comes from the rules
   of "kindness" and "justice"
If you need rules to be kind and just,
   if you *act* virtuous,
   this is a sure sign that virtue is absent
Thus we see the great hypocrisy

Only when the family loses its harmony
   do we hear of "dutiful sons"
Only when the state is in chaos
   do we hear of "loyal ministers"

Verse 19

Abandon holiness
Discard cleverness
    and the people will benefit a hundredfold
Abandon the rules of "kindness"
Discard "righteous" actions
    and the people will return
      to their own natural affections
Abandon book learning
Discard the rules of behavior
    and the people will have no worries
Abandon plots and schemes
Discard profit-seeking
    and the people will not become thieves

These lessons are mere elaborations
The essence of my teachings is this:
    See with original purity
    Embrace with original simplicity
    Reduce what you have
    Decrease what you want

Verse 20

The difference between a formal "yes"
    and a casual "yeah"—how slight!
The difference between knowing the Truth
    and not knowing it—how great!

Must I fear what others fear?
Should I fear desolation
    when there is abundance?
Should I fear darkness
    when that light is shining everywhere?
Nonsense!
The people of this world are steeped in their merrymaking
    as if gorging at a great feast
    or watching the sights of springtime
Yet here I sit, without a sign,
    staring blank-eyed like a child

I am but a guest in this world
While others rush about to get things done
    I accept what is offered
Oh, my mind is like that of a fool
    aloof to the clamor of life around me
Everyone seems so bright and alive
    with the sharp distinctions of day

I appear dark and dull
   with the blending of differences by night

I am drifting like an ocean, floating like the high winds
Everyone is so rooted in this world
   yet I have no place to rest my head
Indeed I am different. . . .
   I have no treasure but the Eternal Mother
   I have no food but what comes from her breast

Verse 21

Perfect action,
True virtue,
Supreme power,
This is how Tao is revealed
   through those who follow it completely

無

Though formless and intangible
   It gives rise to form
Though vague and elusive
   It gives rise to shapes
Though dark and obscure
   It is the spirit, the essence,
   the life-breath of all things
"But is it real?" you ask—
   I say its evidence is all of creation!

名

From the first moment to the present
   The Name has been sounding
It is the gate
   through which the universe enters
The witness
   by which the universe sees

How have I come to know all this?
That very Name has told me,
That Name which is sounding right here,
    right now

Verse 22

"Surrender brings perfection"
The crooked become straight
The empty become full
The worn become new
    Have little and gain much
    Have much and be confused

So the Sage embraces the One
    and becomes a model for the world
Without showing himself, he shines forth
Without promoting himself, he is distinguished
Without claiming reward, he gains endless merit
Without seeking glory, his glory endures

The Sage knows how to follow
    so he comes to command
He does not compete
    so no one under Heaven can compete with him

The ancient saying,
    "Surrender brings perfection,"
    is not just empty words
Truly, surrender brings perfection
    and perfection brings the whole universe

Verse 23

Speak little
Hold to your own nature
A strong wind does not blow all morning
A cloudburst does not last all day
The wind and rain are from Heaven and Earth
    and even these do not last long
How much less so the efforts of man?

One who lives in accordance with the Truth
    becomes the embodiment of Tao
His actions become those of Nature
    his ways those of Heaven
It is through such a one
    that Heaven rejoices
    that Earth rejoices
    that all of life rejoices

Verse 24

On his tiptoes a man is not steady
Taking long strides he cannot keep pace

To the self-serving, nothing shines forth
To the self-promoting, nothing is distinguished
To the self-appointing, nothing bears fruit
To the self-righteous, nothing endures

From the viewpoint of Tao, this self-indulgence
    is like rotting food and painful growths on the body—
Things that all creatures despise
So why hold onto them?
When walking the path of Tao
    this is the very stuff
    that must be uprooted, thrown out, and left behind

Verse 25

Something formless, complete in itself
There before Heaven and Earth
Tranquil, vast, standing alone, unchanging
It provides for all things yet cannot be exhausted
It is the mother of the universe
I do not know its name
    so I call it "Tao"
Forced to name it further
I call it
    "The greatness of all things"
    "The end of all endings"
I call it
    "That which is beyond the beyond"
    "That to which all things return"

道

From Tao comes all greatness—
    It makes Heaven great
    It makes Earth great
    It makes man great

Mankind depends on the laws of Earth
Earth depends on the laws of Heaven
Heaven depends on the laws of Tao
But Tao depends on itself alone
    Supremely free, self-so, it rests in its own nature

Verse 26

The inner is foundation of the outer
The still is master of the restless

The Sage travels all day
    yet never leaves his inner treasure
Though the views are captivating and beg attention
    he remains calm and uninvolved
Tell me, does the lord of a great empire
    go out begging for rice?

One who seeks his treasure in the outer world
    is cut off from his own roots
Without roots, he becomes restless
Being restless, his mind is weak
And with a mind such as this
    he loses all command below Heaven

Verse 27

A knower of the Truth
   travels without leaving a trace
   speaks without causing harm
   gives without keeping an account
The door he shuts, though having no lock,
   cannot be opened
The knot he ties, though using no cord,
   cannot be undone

同

The Sage is always on the side of virtue
   so everyone around him prospers
He is always on the side of truth
   so everything around him is fulfilled

The path of the Sage is called
   "The Path of Illumination"
He who gives himself to this path
   is like a block of wood
   that gives itself to the chisel—
Cut by cut it is honed to perfection

Only a student who gives himself
    can receive the master's gift
If you think otherwise,
    despite your knowledge, you have blundered

Giving and receiving are one
This is called,
    "The great wonder"
    "The essential mystery"
    "The very heart of all that is true"

Verse 28

Hold your male side with your female side
Hold your bright side with your dull side
Hold your high side with your low side
Then you will be able to hold the whole world

When the opposing forces unite within
    there comes a power abundant in its giving
    and unerring in its effect
Flowing through everything
    It returns one to the First Breath
Guiding everything
    It returns one to No Limits
Embracing everything
    It returns one to the Uncarved Block

When the Block is divided
    it becomes something useful
    and leaders rule with a few pieces of it
But the Sage holds the Block complete
Holding all things within himself
    he preserves the Great Unity
    which cannot be ruled or divided

Verse 29

Those who look down upon this world
  will surely take hold and try to change things
But this is a plan
  I've always seen fail
The world is Tao's own vessel
It is perfection manifest
It cannot be changed
It cannot be improved
For those who go on tampering, it's ruined
For those who try to grasp, it's gone

Allow your life to unfold naturally
Know that it too is a vessel of perfection
Just as you breathe in and breathe out
  Sometimes you're ahead and other times behind
  Sometimes you're strong and other times weak
  Sometimes you're with people and other times alone

To the Sage
  all of life is a movement toward perfection
So what need has he
  for the excessive, the extravagant, or the extreme?

Verse 30

Those who rule in accordance with Tao
    do not use force against the world
For that which is forced is likely to return—
Where armies settle
    Nature offers nothing but briars and thorns
After a great battle has been fought
    the land is cursed, the crops fail,
    the Earth lies stripped of its motherhood

A knower of the Truth does what is called for
    then stops
He uses his strength but does not force things
In the same way
    complete your task
    seek no reward
    make no claims
Without faltering
    fully choose to do what you must do
This is to live without forcing
    to overcome without conquering

Things that gain a place by force
    will flourish for a time
    but then fade away
They are not in keeping with Tao
Whatever is not in keeping with Tao
    will come to an early end

Verse 31

Even the finest warrior is defeated
    when he goes against natural law
By his own hand he is doomed
    and all creatures are likely to despise him

One who knows Tao
    never turns from life's calling
When at home he honors the side of rest
When at war he honors the side of action
Peace and tranquility are what he holds most dear
    so he does not obtain weapons
But when their use is unavoidable
    he employs them with fortitude and zeal

Do not flaunt your excellence
Do not rejoice over victory
With the loss of others
    weep with sorrow and grief
After winning a battle
    do not celebrate,
        observe the rites of a funeral

One who is bound to action, proud of victory,
    and delights in the misfortune of others
will never gain a thing
    from this world below Heaven

Verse 32

Tao is eternal, one without a second
Simple indeed
    yet so subtle that no one can master it
If princes and kings could just hold it
All things would flock to their kingdom
Heaven and Earth would rejoice
    with the dripping of sweet dew
Everyone would live in harmony,
        not by official decree,
        but by their own inner goodness

This world is nothing but the glory of Tao
        expressed through different names and forms
One who sees the things of this world
        as being real and self-existent
        has lost sight of the truth
To him, every word becomes a trap
        every thing becomes a prison

One who knows the truth
        that underlies all things
        lives in this world without danger
To him, every word reflects the universe
        every moment brings enlightenment

Rivers and streams are born of the ocean
All creation is born of Tao
Just as all water flows back to become the ocean
All creation flows back to become Tao

Verse 33

One who knows others is intelligent
One who knows himself is enlightened

One who conquers others is strong
One who conquers himself is all-powerful

One who approaches life with force
    surely gets something
One who remains content where he is
    surely gets everything

One who gives himself to his position
    surely lives long
One who gives himself to Tao
    surely lives forever

Verse 34

The great Tao flows everywhere
It fills everything to the left
    and to the right
All things owe their existence to it
    and it cannot deny any one of them

Tao is eternal
It does not favor one over the other
It brings all things to completion
    without their even knowing it

Tao nourishes and protects all creatures
    yet does not claim lordship over them
So we class it with the most humble
Tao is the home to which all things return
    yet it wants nothing in return
So we call it "The Greatest"

The Sage is the same way—
    He does not claim greatness over anything
    He's not even aware of his own greatness
Tell me, what could be greater than this?

Verse 35

Hold fast to the Great Form within
    and let the world pass as it may
Then the changes of life will not bring pain
    but contentment, joy, and well-being

Music and sweets are passing pleasures
    yet they cause people to stop
How bland and insipid are the things of this world
    when one compares them with Tao!
One tastes, but the sweetness turns bitter
One sees, but the colors grow faint
One hears, but the sound fades into silence

One may look for fulfillment in this world
    but his longings will never be exhausted
The only thing he ever finds
    is that he himself is exhausted

Verse 36

Contraction pulls at that
    which extends too far
Weakness pulls at that
    which strengthens too much
Ruin pulls at that
    which rises too high
Loss pulls at life
    when you fill it with too much stuff

The lesson here is called
"The wisdom of obscurity"—
    The gentle outlast the strong
    The obscure outlast the obvious
Hence, a fish that ventures from deep water
    is soon snagged by a net
A country that reveals its strength
    is soon conquered by an enemy

Verse 37

Tao does not act
    yet it is the root of all action
Tao does not move
    yet it is the source of all creation

If princes and kings could hold it
    everyone under them would naturally turn within
Should a doubt or old desire rise up
    The Nameless Simplicity would push it down
The Nameless Simplicity frees the heart of desire
    and reveals its inner silence

When there is silence
    one finds peace
When there is silence
    one finds the anchor of the universe within himself

Verse 38

To give without seeking reward
To help without thinking it is virtuous—
    therein lies great virtue
To keep account of your actions
To help with the hope of gaining merit—
    therein lies no virtue

The highest virtue is to act without a sense of self
The highest kindness is to give without condition
The highest justice is to see without preference

When Tao is lost one must learn the rules of virtue
When virtue is lost, the rules of kindness
When kindness is lost, the rules of justice
When justice is lost, the rules of conduct
And when the high-blown rules of conduct are not followed
    people are seized by the arm and it is forced on them
The rules of conduct
    are just an outer show of devotion and loyalty—
    quite confusing to the heart
And when men rely on these rules for guidance—
    Oh, what ignorance abounds!

The great master follows his own nature
    and not the trappings of life
It is said,
    "He stays with the fruit and not the fluff"
    "He stays with the firm and not the flimsy"
    "He stays with the true and not the false"

Verse 39

From ancient times till now
    the One has been the source of all attainments
By realizing the One
    Heaven becomes clear, Earth becomes still
    spirits gain power and hearts fill up with joy
By realizing the One
    kings and lords become instruments of peace
    and all creatures live joyfully upon this earth
Without the One
    Heaven has no clarity and would crack
    Earth has no peace and would crumble
    spirits have no power and would lose their charm
Without the One
    hearts would dry up, empires would fall,
    all things would go lifelessly upon this earth

地

Long ago kings and lords called themselves
    "orphaned," "lonely," and "unworthy"
What honor can there be without humility?
    What heights can be reached without being low?

The pieces of a chariot are useless
      unless they work in accordance with the whole
A man's life brings nothing
      unless he lives in accordance with the whole universe
Playing one's part
      in accordance with the universe
      is true humility

So whether you're a gem in the royal court
      or a stone on the common path
If you accept your part with humility
      the glory of the universe will be yours

Verse 40

The movement of Tao is to return
The way of Tao is to yield

Heaven, Earth, and all things
    are born of the existent world
The existent world is born of the nothingness of Tao

Verse 41

When the best seeker hears of Tao
 he strives with great effort to know it
When an average seeker hears of Tao
 he thinks of it now and again
When the poorest seeker hears of Tao
 he laughs out loud

Tao is always becoming
 what we have need for it to become
If it could not do this
 it would not be Tao

母

There is an old saying,
 The clear way seems clouded
 The straight way seems crooked
 The sure way seems unsteady

The greatest power seems weak
The purest white seems tainted
The abundant seems empty
The stable seems shaky
The certain seems false
The Great Square has no corners
The Great Vessel is never filled

A beginner may be clumsy
    but after practice—what talent!
A large drum may sit silently
    but when banged—what noise!
Tao lies hidden
    yet it alone is the glorious light of this world

Verse 42

Tao gives life to the one
The one gives life to the two
The two give life to the three
The three give life to ten thousand things

All beings support *yin* and embrace *yang*
    and the interplay of these two forces
    fills the universe
Yet only at the still-point,
    between the breathing in and the breathing out,
    can one capture these two in perfect harmony

無

People suffer at the thought of being
    without parents, without food, or without worth
Yet this is the very way that
    kings and lords once described themselves

Who knows what fate may bring—
    one day your loss may be your fortune
    one day your fortune may be your loss

The age-old lesson that others teach, I also teach—
    "As you plant, so you reap"
    "As you live, so you die"
Know this to be the foundation of my teachings

Verse 43

The most yielding thing in the world
    will overcome the most rigid
The most empty thing in the world
    will overcome the most full
From this comes a lesson—
    Stillness benefits more than action
    Silence benefits more than words

Rare indeed are those who are still
Rare indeed are those who are silent
And so I say,
    Rare indeed are those
    who obtain the bounty of this world

Verse 44

One's own reputation—why the fuss?
One's own wealth—why the concern?
I say, what you gain
    is more trouble than what you lose

Love is the fruit of sacrifice
Wealth is the fruit of generosity

Be content,
    rest in your own fullness—
You will not suffer from loss
You'll avoid the snare of this world
You'll have long life and endless blessings

Verse 45

The Great Perfection seems imperfect
    yet this world it creates is never impaired
The Great Fullness seems empty
    yet this world it creates is never lacking

Great truth seems false
Great skill seems clumsy
Great eloquence seems like babble

Keep moving and you'll miss the cold
Keep silent and you'll beat the heat

Be tranquil like the rain of spring
Be pure like the sheen of silk
Then the Great Perfection will be perfect
    and the Great Fullness will be full

Verse 46

When Tao is present in the empire
    men follow their own nature
    and riding horses work the fields
When Tao is absent from the empire
    men go astray
    and war horses breed on sacred ground

There is no greater loss than losing Tao
    No greater curse than desire
    No greater tragedy than discontentment
    No greater fault than selfishness

Contentment alone is enough
Indeed, the bliss of eternity
    can be found in your contentment

Verse 47

Without going outside
    one can know the whole world
Without looking out the window
    one can see the ways of Heaven
The farther one goes
    the less one knows

Thus the Sage does not go, yet he knows
    He does not look, yet he sees
    He does not do, yet all is done

Verse 48

To become learned, gain daily
To obtain Tao, reduce daily
Reduce and reduce again
    until all action is reduced to non-action
Then no one is left
Nothing is done
    yet nothing is left undone

One who gives freely and without attachment
    gets a full life in return
One who gives with the secret hope of getting
    is merely engaged in business
Truly, they neither give nor receive
    any of the treasure from this world below Heaven

Verse 49

The Sage has no fixed heart of his own
Those who look at him
    see their own hearts

Those who are good he treats with goodness
Those who are bad he also treats with goodness
    because the nature of his being is good
Those who are truthful he treats with truth
Those who are not truthful he also treats with truth
    because the nature of his being is truthful

The Sage lives in harmony with all below Heaven
He sees everything as his own self
He loves everyone as his own child
All people are drawn to him
    every eye and ear is turned toward him

Verse 50

Again and again
Men come in with birth
   and go out with death
One in three are followers of life
One in three are followers of death
And those just passing from life to death
   also number one in three
But they all die in the end
Why is this so?
Because they clutch to life
   and cling to this passing world

I hear that one who lives by his own truth
   is not like this
He walks without making footprints in this world
Going about, he does not fear the rhinoceros or tiger
Entering a battlefield, he does not fear sharp weapons
For in him the rhino can find no place to pitch its horn
The tiger no place to fix its claw
The soldier no place to thrust his blade
Why is this so?
Because he dwells in that place
   where death cannot enter

Verse 51

Tao gives all things life
   Te gives them fulfillment
Nature is what shapes them
Living is what brings them to completion
Every creature honors Tao and worships Te
   not by force
   but through its own living and breathing

Though Tao gives life to all things
   Te is what cultivates them
Te is that magic power that
   raises and rears them
   completes and prepares them
   comforts and protects them

To create without owning
To give without expecting
To fill without claiming
   This is the profound action of Tao
   The highest expression of Te

Verse 52

That which creates the universe
    is the Mother of the world
By knowing the Mother
    one knows her children
By knowing her children
    one comes to know her
Such is their unity
    that one does not exist without the other

Fully embrace your life
    and you will share in the glory of creation
The Mother herself will be your guardian
And all her creation will be your guide

Stay with the Mother, shut the mouth, close the gates
    and you are never in trouble
Abandon the Mother, open the mouth, be busy with others
    and you are beyond all hope of rescue

Seeing your own smallness is called insight
Honoring your own tenderness is called strength

The sun in all its glory
    reveals but a passing world
Only the inner light illumines eternity
Only that light can guide us back home

Have faith
Follow your own shining
Be aware of your own awareness
On the darkest nights you will not stumble
On the brightest days you will not blink
This is called
    "The Practice of Eternal Light"

Verse 53

If I had the least bit of wisdom
    I could follow the path of Tao quite well
My only fear would be trying to go my own way
The Great Path is simple and direct
    yet people love to take the side-routes

See how magnificent the courts have become
The women dress in colorful gowns
The men carry well-crafted swords
Food and drink overflow
Wealth and finery abound
Yet in the shadow of all this splendor
    the fields grow barren
    the granaries are all but empty

I say this pomp at the expense of others
    is like the boasting of thieves after a looting
Surely it is contrary to Tao
Surely it cuts against the grain of the whole empire

Verse 54

Truth, once established, can never be uprooted
Goodness, once imbibed, can never be stripped away
    A sacrifice to a higher cause is never lost
    An offering to an ancestor never goes to waste

When a person embodies Tao
    his heart becomes true
When a family embodies Tao
    it thrives
When a village embodies Tao
    it is protected
When a country embodies Tao
    it prospers
When the world embodies Tao
    it reveals its perfection

Tao is everywhere
    it has become everything
To truly see it, see it as it is
In a person, see it *as* a person
In a family, see it *as* a family
In a country, see it *as* a country
In the world, see it *as* the world

How have I come to know all this?
Tao has shown me—
    Tao as all this!

Verse 55

One who embraces Tao
    will become pure and innocent
    like a newborn babe
Deadly insects will not sting him
Wild beasts will not attack him
Birds of prey will not strike him
He is oblivious to the union of male and female
    yet his vitality is full
    his inner spirit is complete
He can cry all day without straining
    so perfect is his harmony
    so magically does he blend with this world

Know this harmony—it brings the Eternal
Know the Eternal—it brings enlightenment

A full life—this is your blessing
A gentle heart—this is your strength

Things in harmony with Tao remain
Things that are forced, grow for a while
    but then wither away
This is not Tao
Whatever is not Tao
    comes to an early end

Verse 56

One who speaks does not know
One who knows does not speak

Shut the mouth
Close the gates
Blunt the sharpness
Loosen the knots
Temper the glare
Become one with the dust of the world
This is called
    "The Secret Embrace"

One who knows this secret
    is not moved by attachment or aversion,
    swayed by profit or loss,
    nor touched by honor or disgrace
He is far beyond the cares of men
    yet comes to hold the dearest place in their hearts

Verse 57

To rule the state, have a known plan
To win a battle, have an unknown plan
To gain the universe, have no plan at all

Let the universe itself
    reveal to you its splendor
How do I know this should be so?
    Because of this—
The more restrictions, the more poverty
The more weapons, the more fear in the land
The more cleverness, the more strange events
The more laws, the more lawbreakers

Thus the Sages say,
    Act with a pure heart and the people will be transformed
    Love your own life and the people will be uplifted
    Give without conditions and the people will prosper
    Want nothing and the people will find everything

Verse 58

When the ruler knows his own heart
    the people are simple and pure
When he meddles with their lives
    they become restless and disturbed

有

Bad fortune, yes—
    it rests upon good fortune
Good fortune, yes—
    it hides within bad fortune
Oh the things that Heaven sends—
    Who can know their final aim?
    Who can tell of their endless ways?
Today the righteous turn to trickery
Tomorrow the good turn to darkness
Oh what delusion abounds
    and every day it grows worse!

But the Sage is here upon the Earth
    to gently guide us back
He cuts but does not harm
He straightens but does not disrupt
He illumines but does not dazzle

Verse 59

Rule the people and serve Heaven
    yet hold nothing more dear than the Mother's harvest
Let every thought and every breath
    be the fruit of your offering—
Do it now
Let her power run thick in your blood
    There will be no obstacle you cannot overcome
    No limit you cannot surpass
    No empire you cannot rule

Ah, but in all your glory
    never lose sight of the Mother
Without her
    your empire will crumble
    your power will waste away
For the Mother brings the harvest
    She alone causes all things to endure

We call this
    "Deep roots and a solid trunk"
    "The way of long life and lasting insight"

Verse 60

Govern a nation as you would fry a small fish

山

When Tao is present in the empire
    dark spirits lose their power
It's not that they have no power
    it's that their power can't harm anyone
When Tao is present
    the people enjoy the blessings of Heaven
They find unity
They find peace

What's this about spirits doing harm?
The Sage is approaching
    and they are rushing in to sweep his path!

Verse 61

A great state is like a river basin
    that receives everything flowing into it
It is the place where all things come to rest
    where all the world is welcomed

The low is greater than the high
The still is greater than the restless
    The low country wins over its neighbor
    The still female wins over the male

The Sage wants to uplift the people
The people want to follow the Sage
    only by being low does this come to be
The Sage bows to the people
The people bow to the Sage
And when they lift up their heads
    only greatness remains

Verse 62

Tao is the treasure-house
   the true nature
   the secret source of everything
It is the great wealth of those who are awake
   the great protector of those still sleeping

If a person seems wicked
   do not cast him away—
Awaken him with your words
Elevate him with your deeds
Requite his injury with your kindness
Do not cast him away
   cast away his wickedness

欲

When the emperor is crowned
   or the three ministers installed
   they receive a gift of jade and horses
But how can this compare
   to sitting still and gaining the treasure of Tao
This is why the ancient masters
   honored the inward path of Tao

Did they not say
    "Seek and you will find"?
    "Err and you will be forgiven"?
Within, within
This is where the world's treasure has always been

Verse 63

Act without acting
Give without giving
Taste without tasting

Tao alone becomes all things great and all things small
It is the One in many
It is the many in One

Let Tao become all your actions
 then your wants will become your treasure
 your injury will become your blessing

後

Take on difficulties while they are still easy
Do great things while they are still small
Step by step the world's burden is lifted
Piece by piece the world's treasure is amassed

So the Sage stays with his daily task
 and accomplishes the greatest thing
Beware of those who promise a quick and easy way
 for much ease brings many difficulties

Follow your path to the end
Accept difficulty as an opportunity
This is the sure way to end up
 with no difficulties at all

Verse 64

A still mind can easily hold the truth
The difficulties yet to come can easily be avoided

The feeble are easily broken
The small are easily scattered
Begin your task before it becomes a burden
Put things in order before they get out of hand
Remember,
A tree that fills a man's embrace grows from a seedling
A tower nine stories high starts with one brick
A journey of a thousand miles begins with a single step

出

Act and it's ruined
Grab and it's gone
People on the verge of success often lose patience
        and fail in their undertakings
Be steady from the beginning to the end
        and you won't bring on failure

同

The Sage desires that which has no desires
        and teaches that which cannot be taught
He does not value the objects held by a few
        but only that which is held by everyone

He guides men back to their own treasure
   and helps all things come to know
   the truth they have forgotten
All this he does without a stir

Verse 65

The ancient ones were simple-hearted
　　and blended with the common people
They did not shine forth
They did not rule with cleverness
　　So the nation was blessed

Now the rulers are filled with clever ideas
　　and the lives of people are filled with hardship
　　So the nation is cursed

道

He who knows the play of Tao and Te
　　knows the nature of the universe
Tao brings forth Te from its own being
Te expands in all directions
　　filling every corner of the world
　　becoming the splendor of all creation
Yet at every moment Te seeks Tao
This is the movement that guides the universe
This is the impulse
　　that leads all things back home

Verse 66

Why do the hundred rivers
    turn and rush toward the sea?
Because it naturally stays below them

He who wishes to rule over the people
    must speak as if below them
He who wishes to lead the people
    must walk as if behind them
So the Sage rules over the people
    but he does not weigh them down
He leads the people
    but he does not block their way

The Sage stays low
    so the world never tires of exalting him
He remains a servant
    so the world never tires of making him its king

Verse 67

All the world talks about my Tao
  with such familiarity—
What folly!
Tao is not something found at the marketplace
  or passed on from father to son
It is not something gained by knowing
  or lost by forgetting
If Tao were like this
It would have been lost and forgotten long ago

玄

I have three treasures that I cherish and hold dear
  the first is love
  the second is moderation
  the third is humility
With love one is fearless
With moderation one is abundant
With humility one can fill the highest position
Now if one is fearless but has no love
  abundant but has no moderation
  rises up but has no humility
Surely he is doomed

Love vanquishes all attackers
It is impregnable in defense
When Heaven wants to protect someone
  does it send an army?
No, it protects him with love

Verse 68

The best warrior
　　leads without haste
　　fights without anger
　　overcomes without confrontation
He puts himself below
　　and brings out the highest in his men

This is the virtue of not confronting
　　of working with the abilities you have
　　of complying with the laws of Heaven

This is the ancient path that leads to perfection

Verse 69

The great warriors have a saying,
"I dare not act as host
    but would rather be a guest
I dare not advance an inch
    but would rather retreat a foot"

So advance but do not use your feet
Seize but do not use your arms
Cut but do not use your sword
Fight but do not use your own power

There is no greater misfortune than feeling
    "I have an enemy"
For when "I" and "enemy" exist together
    there is no room left for my treasure

Thus, when two opponents meet
    the one without an enemy
    will surely triumph

Verse 70

My teachings are very easy to understand
 and very easy to practice
Yet so few in this world understand
 and so few are able to practice

My words arise from that ancient source
My actions are those of the universe itself
If people do not know these
 how can they know me?

Those who follow my ways are rare
 and so I treasure them
Even if they wear the clothes of a beggar
 they carry a priceless gem within

Verse 71

Knowing what cannot be known—
    what a lofty aim!
Not knowing what needs to be known—
    what a terrible result!

Only when your sickness becomes sick
    will your sickness disappear

The Sage's illness has become ill
    his renunciation has been renounced
Now he is free
And every place in this world
    is the perfect place to be

Verse 72

When the people do not fear worldly power
    a greater power will arrive

Don't limit the view of yourself
Don't despise the conditions of your birth
Don't resist the natural course of your life
    In this way you will never weary of this world

The Sage knows himself, but not as himself
    he loves himself, but not as himself
    he honors himself, but not as himself
Thus, he discards the view of his own self
    and chooses the view of the universe

Verse 73

Bold action against others leads to death
Bold action in harmony with Tao leads to life

非

Good fortune, bad fortune
One seems to bring benefit
   the other to cause harm
But Heaven rejects them both
Both, in the end, tether men to this world

Who can know the reasons of Heaven?
   Who can know its endless ways?
Not even the Sage has an answer to this one

門

Heaven's way does not strive
   yet it always overcomes
It does not speak, yet it responds
It is not summoned, yet it appears
It does not hurry, yet it completes everything on time

The net of Heaven spans the universe
   yet not the slightest thing ever slips by

Verse 74

If people do not fear death
    why threaten them with it?
But suppose they did fear death
    and this was the fate handed to lawbreakers
Who would dare to do the killing?

There is always a Lord of Death
He who takes the place of the Lord of Death
    is like one who cuts with the blade
    of a master carpenter
Whoever cuts with the blade of a master carpenter
    is sure to cut his own hands

Verse 75

Why are the people starving?—
   Because their grain is being eaten up by taxes
   That's why they're starving

Why are the people rebellious?—
   Because those above them meddle in their lives
   That's why they're rebellious

Why do the people regard death so lightly?—
   Because they are so involved with their own living
   That's why they regard death so lightly

In the end,
The treasure of life is missed by those who hold on
   and gained by those who let go

Verse 76

When life begins
   we are tender and weak
When life ends
   we are stiff and rigid
All things, including the grass and trees,
   are soft and pliable in life
   dry and brittle in death

So the soft and supple
   are the companions of life
While the stiff and unyielding
   are the companions of death

An army that cannot yield
   will be defeated
A tree that cannot bend
   will crack in the wind
Thus by Nature's own decree
   the hard and strong are defeated
   while the soft and gentle are triumphant

Verse 77

Heaven operates like the bending of a bow—
 the high it pulls down
 the low it brings up
It takes from that which has too much
And gives to that which has too little
The way of man is otherwise—
 he takes from that which is depleted
 and gives to that which has too much

Who can offer an abundance to the world?—
One who has Tao
Such a one can give like the heavens

The Sage gives
 without relying on his own effort
He completes
 without waiting for reward
He illumines
 without stepping from the shadow

Verse 78

Nothing in this world
    is as soft and yielding as water
Yet for attacking the hard and strong
    none can triumph so easily
It is weak, yet none can equal it
It is soft, yet none can damage it
It is yielding, yet none can wear it away

Everyone knows that the soft overcomes the hard
    and the yielding triumphs over the rigid
Why then so little faith?
Why can no one practice it?

So the Sages say,
    fulfill even the lowest position
    love even the weakest creature
Then you will be called
    "Lord of every offering"
    "King of all below Heaven"

Verse 79

After settling a great dispute
    some resentment is sure to remain
Being content with what you have
    is always best in the end

The Sage always assumes the debt
    as if holding the left side of a contract
He gives and gives, and wants nothing in return

One with true virtue
    always seeks a way to give
One who lacks true virtue
    always seeks a way to get
To the giver comes the fullness of life
    to the taker just an empty hand

Though the Tao of Heaven has no favorites
    it always sides with one who has a pure heart

Verse 80

Let every state be simple
　　like a small village with few people
There may be tools to speed things up
　　ten or a hundred times
　　yet no one will care to use them
There may be boats and carriages
　　yet they will remain without riders
There may be armor and weaponry
　　yet they will sit collecting dust

The people must take death seriously
　　and not waste their lives in distant lands
Let them return
　　to the knotting of cord
Let them enjoy their food
　　and care for their clothing
Let them be content in their homes
　　and joyful in the way they live

Neighboring villages are within sight of each other
Roosters and dogs can be heard in the distance
Should a man grow old and die
　　without ever leaving his village
　　let him feel as though there was nothing he missed

Verse 81

Words born of the mind are not true
True words are not born of the mind

Those who have virtue do not look for faults
Those who look for faults have no virtue

Those who come to know It
    do not rely on learning
Those who rely on learning
    do not come to know It

玄

The Sage sees the world
    as an expansion of his own self
So what need has he to accumulate things?
By giving to others
    he gains more and more
By serving others
    he receives everything

Heaven gives,
   and all things turn out for the best
The Sage lives,
   and all things go as Tao goes
   all things move as the wind blows

About the Author

Jonathan Star has been widely acclaimed for his poetic and mystical translations of Rumi, Hafez, and the poet-saints of India. His previous works include *Rumi: In the Arms of the Beloved, A Garden Beyond Paradise,* and *The Inner Treasure.* He lives in upstate New York.

TARCHER
PENGUIN

FIND YOURSELF IN TARCHER CORNERSTONE EDITIONS . . .

a powerful new line of keepsake trade paperbacks that highlight the foundational works of ancient and modern spiritual literature.

The Essential Marcus Aurelius

Newly translated and introduced by Jacob Needleman and John P. Piazza

A stunningly relevant and reliable translation of the thoughts and aphorisms of the Stoic philosopher and Roman emperor Marcus Aurelius.

January 2008   ISBN 978-1-58542-617-1

Tao Te Ching

The New Translation from *Tao Te Ching: The Definitive Edition*
Lao Tzu, translated by Jonathan Star

"It would be hard to find a fresh approach to a text that ranks only behind the Bible as the most widely translated book in the world, but Star achieves that goal."

—NAPRA ReView

January 2008   ISBN 978-1-58542-618-8

Accept This Gift
Selections from *A Course in Miracles*
Edited by Frances Vaughan, Ph.D., and Roger Walsh, M.D., Ph.D.
Foreword by Marianne Williamson

"An invaluable collection from one of the great sources of the perennial wisdom—a gold mine of psychological and spiritual insights."

—KEN WILBER

January 2008   ISBN 978-1-58542-619-5

The Kybalion
Three Initiates

Who wrote this mysterious guide to the principles of esoteric psychology and worldly success? History has kept readers guessing. . . . Experience for yourself the intriguing ideas of an underground classic.

May 2008   ISBN 978-1-58542-643-0

The Spiritual Emerson
Ralph Waldo Emerson, introduction by Jacob Needleman

This concise volume collects the core writings that have made Ralph Waldo Emerson a key source of insight for spiritual seekers of every faith—with an introduction by the bestselling philosopher Jacob Needleman.

July 2008   ISBN 978-1-58542-642-3